"That woman must be on drugs."

"That woman must be on drugs."

A Collection of Sylvia by Nicole Hollander

St. Martin's Press, New York

Library of Congress Cataloging in Publication Data

Hollander, Nicole.
  That woman must be on drugs.

  A collection of Sylvia cartoons.
  I.   Women—Caricatures and cartoons. II.   American
wit and humor, pictorial. I. Sylvia (Comic strip)
  II.   Title.
NC1429.H588A4 1981   741.5′973   80-28882
ISBN 0-312-79510-6 (pbk)

Copyright © 1981 by Nicole Hollander
For information, write: St. Martin's Press,
175 Fifth Avenue, New York, N.Y. 10010
Manufactured in the United States of America

10 9 8 7 6 5

*Book designed by Tom Greensfelder
    and Nicole Hollander
Jacket photo by Donna Dunlap*

Who is Sylvia? What is she,
That all the swains commend her?
Holy, fair, and wise is she;
The heaven such grace did lend her,
That she might admired be.

Two Gentleman of Verona - Wm. Shakespeare

LOSS OF
CONSCIOUSNESS.

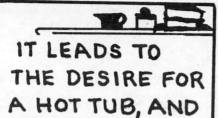

IT LEADS TO THE DESIRE FOR A HOT TUB, AND TO A PREOCCU-PATION WITH KARMA—AND

IN THE FINAL STAGES, 2 WEEKS AT ESALEN.

RITA, I JUST DON'T HAVE THE TIME.

THE TELEPHONE COMPANY HAS A NEW IDEA FOR THE NEW WOMAN.

FOR THE GAL ON THE "GO" WHO HAS NO TIME TO SIT BY THE PHONE WAITING FOR SOME GUY TO CALL.

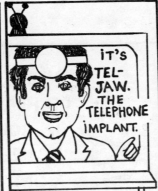

IT'S TEL-JAW. THE TELEPHONE IMPLANT.

WHEN THE PHONE RINGS, YOUR EYES LIGHT UP.

IF WE CAN'T BE LOVERS, WE CAN BE FRIENDS... CAN'T WE?

MAYBE.

ANYTHING AS BORING AS THIS, HAS TO BE BAD FOR YOU.

GOOD. SEE YA.

THERE MUST BE A LINK BETWEEN WATCHING T.V. AND CANCER.

IDEAS FOR TELEVISION GAME SHOWS #1

THE BARRIS GAME

*People compete for prizes and the
chance to publicly humiliate
Chuck Barris.*

ISN'T THE BABY ADORABLE, JACK?

NICOLE HOLLANDER

OH, HOW CAN I TELL HER THAT HER BABY IS REALLY KATRINA'S BABY, AND HER BABY WAS LOST IN THE NURSERY?

SEND HER A SINGING TELEGRAM.

MA, I GOTTA GET IN THERE; I'M GOING TO BE LATE FOR LYDIA'S WEDDING.

DON'T BOTHER. I SAW HER BUYING A ONE-WAY TICKET TO BUENOS AIRES.

BOY YOU'D SAY ANY-THING WOULDN'T YOU?

ANYTHING THE TRAFFIC WILL BEAR.

WHEN DID YOU FIRST REALIZE THAT YOUR SKIN WOULDN'T BE 21 FOREVER?

WAS IT WHEN YOU SAW YOUR TINY LAUGH LINES DEEPEN? OR WHEN YOU FIRST NOTICED A FINE NETWORK OF WRINKLES ON YOUR UPPER LIP? I'D LIKE TO SHARE THE BEAUTY SECRETS THAT HAVE BEEN IN MY FAMILY FOR GENERATIONS WITH YOU—

AND, I'LL SHARE MINE, WITH YOU.

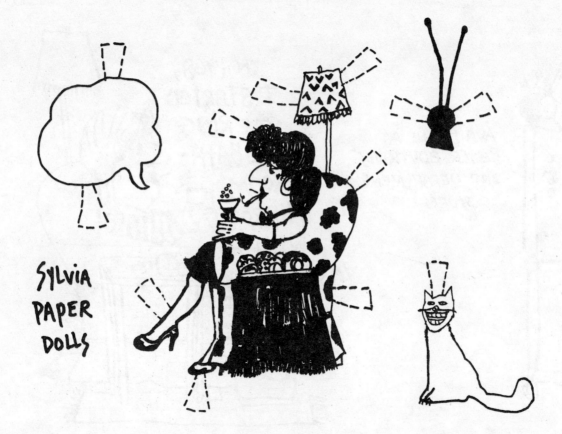

SYLVIA
PAPER
DOLLS

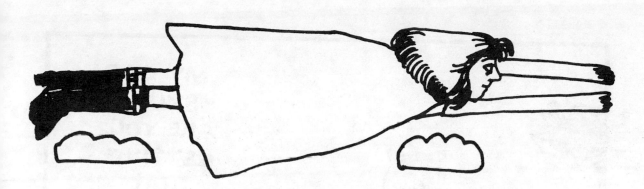

SUPERWOMAN REALIZES THAT SHE DID NOT SET THE TIMER ON HER MICROWAVE OVEN.

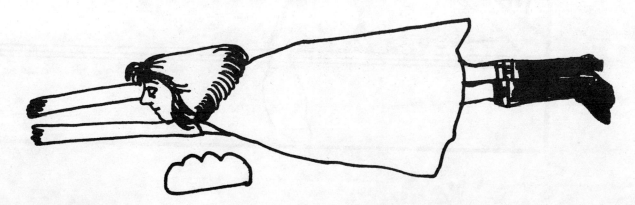

IDEAS FOR TELEVISION GAME SHOWS #2

THE CHILDHOOD GAME

People compete for prizes and a chance to tell lies about their childhoods.

Q: What was your childhood like?

A: It was idyllic. My parents and my brothers and sisters were very close; we were always laughing, there was a lot of love there. In fact I can't remember a harsh word being exchanged. My grandparents both paternal and maternal lived with us, they entertained us with reminiscences of their early days on farms in the midwest. We had quite a number of animals too, and a boat child.

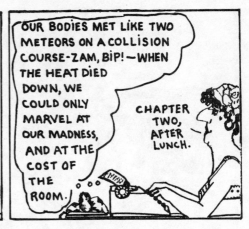

CHANGING ATTITUDES TOWARD CHILDLESS MARRIAGES
CHANGING ATTITUDES TOWARD THE UNMARRIED

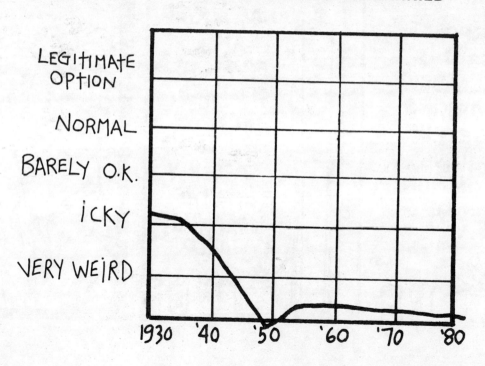

THE THING YOU
REALLY GOT TO
HAND TO WOMEN,
IS THAT THEY ARE
VERY VERBAL.

I MEAN YOUR
AVERAGE WOMAN
CAN WIN YOUR
AVERAGE DOMESTIC
ARGUMENT WITH
A MAN.

WHICH IS WHY
THEY GET
BEAT UP.
ALL THE TIME.

MAN APOLOGIZES TO WIFE

OHIO (UPI)—Late today in Akron, Ohio, a man apologized to his wife for drinking the last Coke in the refrigerator. "You could have knocked me over with a feather," said their next door neighbor.

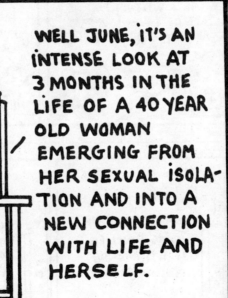

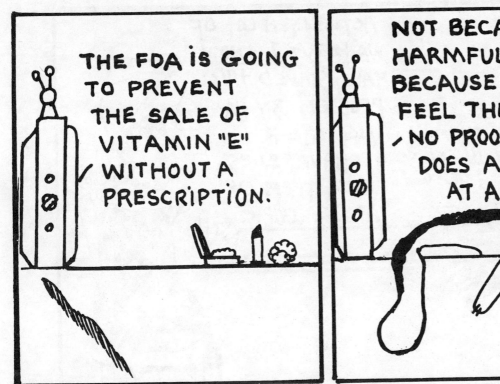

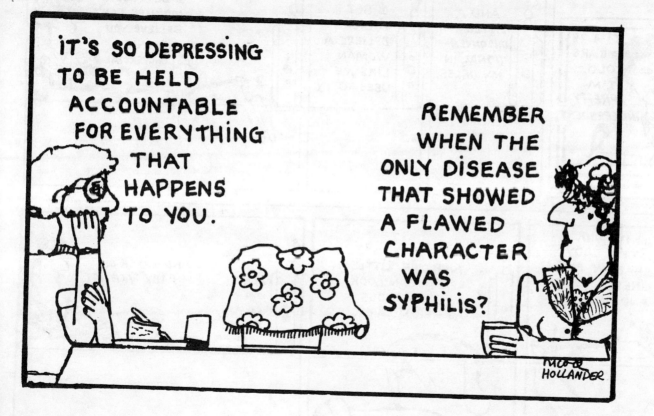

DO YOU HAVE SEXY HANDS?
Match your hands to the ones below

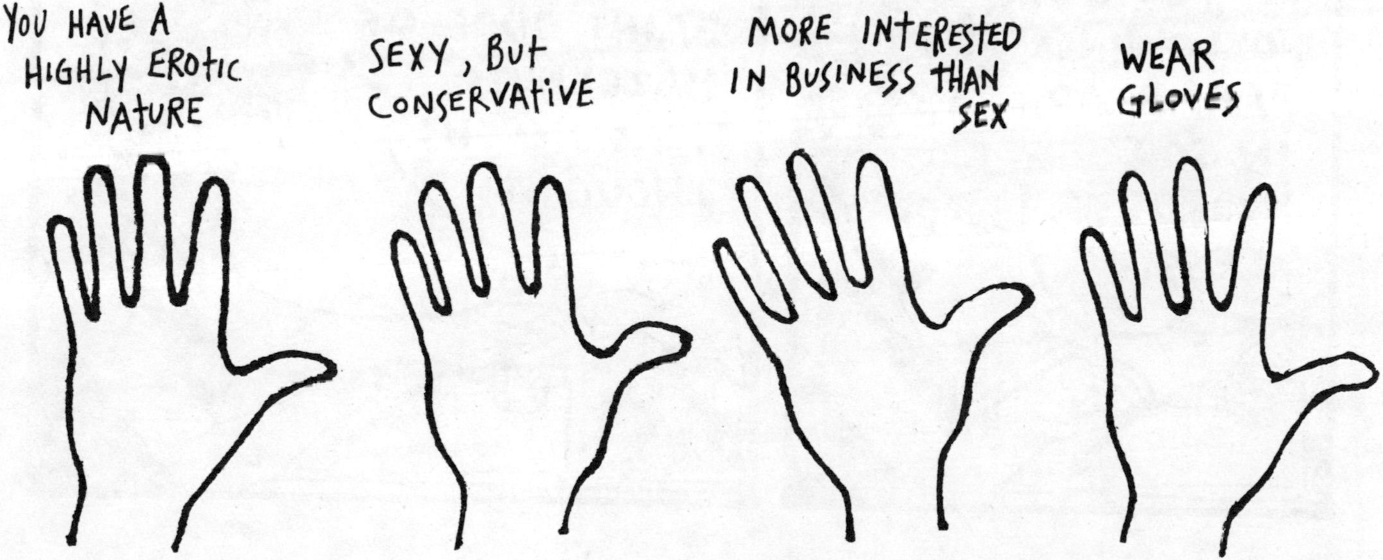

YOU HAVE A
HIGHLY EROTIC
NATURE

SEXY, BUT
CONSERVATIVE

MORE INTERESTED
IN BUSINESS THAN
SEX

WEAR
GLOVES